BRUSH YOUR TEETH!

HEALTHY DENTAL HABITS

Mary Elizabeth Salzmann

Consulting Editor,
Diane Craig, M.A./ Reading Specialist

Sandcastle

An Imprint of Abdo Publishing
www.abdopublishing.com

www.abdopublishing.com

Published by Abdo Publishing, a division of ABDO, PO Box 398166, Minneapolis, Minnesota 55439.
Copyright © 2015 by Abdo Consulting Group, Inc. International copyrights reserved in all countries. No part
of this book may be reproduced in any form without written permission from the publisher. SandCastle™ is a
trademark and logo of Abdo Publishing.

Printed in the United States of America, North Mankato, Minnesota
102014
012015

THIS BOOK CONTAINS
RECYCLED MATERIALS

Editor: Alex Kuskowski
Content Developer: Nancy Tuminelly
Cover and Interior Design: Colleen Dolphin, Mighty Media, Inc.
Photo Credits: Shutterstock

Library of Congress Cataloging-in-Publication Data

Salzmann, Mary Elizabeth, 1968- author.

 Brush your teeth! : healthy dental habits / Mary Elizabeth Salzmann.

    pages cm. -- (Healthy habits)

 Audience: Ages 4-9.

 ISBN 978-1-62403-528-9

1. Teeth--Care and hygiene--Juvenile literature. 2. Dentistry--Juvenile literature. I. Title. II. Series: Salzmann, Mary
Elizabeth, 1968- Healthy habits.

 RK63.S24 2015

 617.6'01--dc23

                        2014023950

SandCastle™ Level: Transitional

SandCastle™ books are created by a team of professional educators, reading specialists, and content developers around
five essential components—phonemic awareness, phonics, vocabulary, text comprehension, and fluency—to assist young
readers as they develop reading skills and strategies and increase their general knowledge. All books are written, reviewed,
and leveled for guided reading, early reading intervention, and Accelerated Reader® programs for use in shared, guided, and
independent reading and writing activities to support a balanced approach to literacy instruction. The SandCastle™ series
has four levels that correspond to early literacy development. The levels are provided to help teachers and parents select
appropriate books for young readers.

EMERGING · BEGINNING · **TRANSITIONAL** · FLUENT

CONTENTS

WHAT IS A HEALTHY HABIT?

Taking care of your teeth is a healthy **habit**.

Taking care of
your teeth helps
prevent **cavities.**

Brush your teeth every day.

Flossing is good for your teeth too.

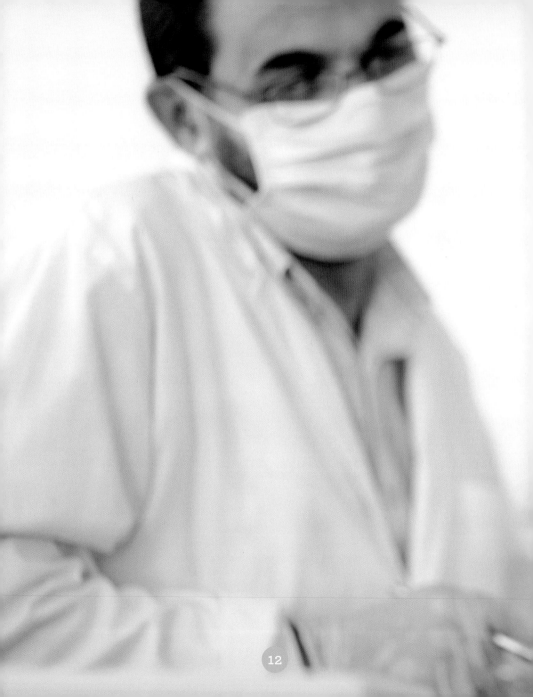

Go to the **dentist** for **checkups.**

13

Lizzie has **braces**.
They straighten
her teeth.

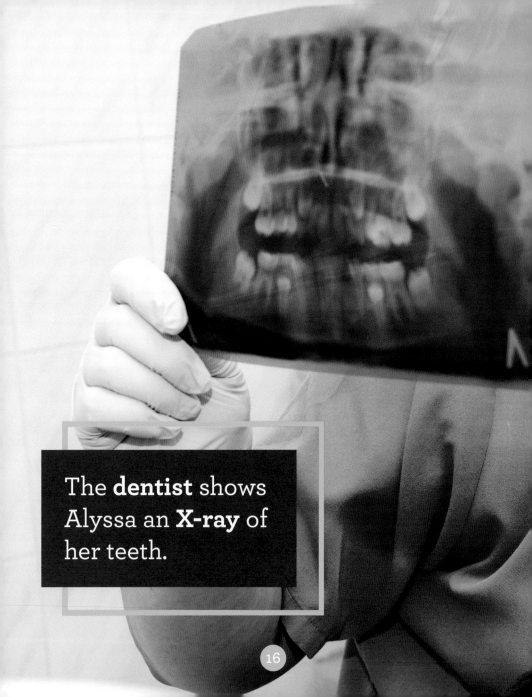

The **dentist** shows Alyssa an **X-ray** of her teeth.

Eric brushes his teeth with his dad.

Jonathan learns the right way to brush his teeth.

How do you take care of your teeth?

HEALTH QUIZ

1. Taking care of your teeth is a healthy **habit**. True or False?

2. You should brush your teeth once a week. True or False?

3. **Flossing** is not good for your teeth. True or False?

4. Eric brushes his teeth with his dad. True or False?

5. Jonathan learns the right way to brush his teeth. True or False?

Answers: 1. True 2. False 3. False 4. True 5. True

23

GLOSSARY

braces – wires and brackets attached to the teeth to straighten them.

cavity – a spot on a tooth that has started to rot or decay.

checkup – a routine exam by a doctor or dentist.

dentist – a person trained to help people take care of their teeth.

floss – to clean between your teeth with special string called dental floss.

habit – a behavior done so often that it becomes automatic.

X-ray – a photograph of the inside of the body or another object.